FINISHING LINE PRESS

www.finishinglinepress.com

HIS ONLY MERIT

poems by

Benjamin Green

Finishing Line Press
Georgetown, Kentucky

HIS ONLY MERIT

ACKNOWLEDGMENTS

Some of these poems appeared, sometimes in different forms, in previous
publications:

"Woman Looking at a Vase of Flowers" in *Plants and Poetry Journal*
"The Poems of our Climate" and "The Auroras of Autumn, II" in *Ocotillo
Review*
"Tea at the Palaz of Hoon" and "World Without Peculiarity" in *Glissando*
"Of the Surface of Things," "The Poems of Our Climate," "Two Illustrations
that the World is What You Make of It," and "Anglais Mort a Florence" in
Pinyon Review
"Domination in Black" in *Lone Mountain Literary Society*
"The Solitude of Cataracts" in *Beyond Words Literary Magazine*
"Autumn Refrain" in *The Raven's Perch*
"Extracts from Addresses to the Academy of Fine Ideas, IV" in
fws: international journal of literature and art
"Not Ideas about the Thing but the Thing Itself" in *Santa Fe Writers Project
Journal* and *The Paddock Review*

Publisher: Leah Huete de Maines
Editor: Christen Kincaid
Cover Art: Benjamin Green
Author Photo: Benjamin Green
Cover Design: Elizabeth Maines McCleavy

Order online: www.finishinglinepress.com
also available on amazon.com

Author inquiries and mail orders:
Finishing Line Press
PO Box 1626
Georgetown, Kentucky 40324
USA

Contents

Introduction

A copy of *The Collected Poems of Wallace Stevens* sat on my shelf for decades. Familiar with his work without having read the collection, I never got around to actually read the book until recently. When I finally read the book, marginalia from a previous owner, penned in a most elegant script, caught my immediate attention. On the fly leaf I read: *Titles herein mean much more than the poems themselves—perhaps that's his only merit!* I borrowed that judgement for my chapbook title and retained Stevens' titles for my own work.

I don't think this previous owner read the entire book; the marginalia ceases on page 128 of the 534-page volume. Some of the comments written in the margins compare Stevens' lines to other authors; I recognized references to Joyce and Yeats and Gibran. Some offer praise: good, *That's clear!, interesting, very nice.* A few label Stevens' themes: *pantheism, human imagination, logical positivism, world as paradise, gotta have earth!* Some are more critical: *what? Big Deal! Has Stevens ever really seen Key West! I doubt it!*

Wallace Stevens, born in 1879, died in 1955 (before my birth). He pursued an elite education that led towards a degree in law. He settled on a career in insurance and although well-traveled, spent most of his adult life in two houses on Farmington Avenue in Hartford, Connecticut. Despite my book's previous owner's doubts, Stevens did spend a great deal of time in Florida, and a fist fight he engaged in with a young Ernest Hemingway in Key West remains the stuff of literary legend. Stevens broke his hand on Hemingway's jaw; the fight ended with Stevens prone on the sidewalk outside the building where the brawl started.

Stevens' first of five books of poetry appeared in 1923, one year after Eliot's *The Waste Land*. Along with Yeats, Eliot and Stevens make up the great trio of modernist poets. Contemporary poets included William Carlos Williams and Robert Frost. Williams remains famous for everyday observations in conversational, free verse language. Frost wrote in plain language also, but within the constraint of rigid metrical schemes. Stevens employed a playful language full of commonplace objects (what Frost referred to as "bric-a-brac") set within an abstract and intellectual vocabulary. Stevens was not well-received, originally, but his critical reception grew over time.

Stevens never introduced himself as a poet to his workmates in insurance and he did not really relate with other poets, but of poetry he wrote that it possessed a "vital significance" that could "propose a fulfillment." He wanted to write the "great poem of the earth," but his poetry always debates what is natural and what is imagined, what is fact and what is image.

I had no intention of writing the great poem of the earth when I started this collection. The nineteen poems from Stevens that I chose as inspiration are not those usually found in anthologies, especially in the earlier major anthologies of American and world poetry. What moved me were the shorter lyrical poems, or sections of the longer works.

Some of the results appear as "after" poems, some compose conversations between poems, some become conversations between poets, some comprise arguments between poets and poems, some express agreements.

I write from a high desert canyon in New Mexico rather than the wintry confines of Hartford or the tropical humidity of Florida. I write from my experience and with my own vocabulary; I cherished the opportunity to borrow a more intellectual and abstract verbiage. Hopefully one reader, at least, will find merit in the poems as well as the titles.

DOMINATION OF BLACK

Under the moon, and faint stars,
The shapes of the junipers
And of the cottonwood leaves
Layer themselves with shadows
And the shadows dance
With the leaves and trees.
Yes! and the bulk of the heavy mesa
Rises ponderously
As I hear the howl of coyotes.
It sounds like three of them.

The music of their cries
Conducts the leaves
And their shadows,
Prompts their dancing in the night,
In the dark night.
The howls fill the canyon
As an owl flies from the dark of a pinyon
Down to the ground to capture a mouse.
I listen, to hoot and howl.
Are they songs to the darkness,
Hymns for the domination of black?
A howl to the leaves and shadows dancing?
A hoot to the moon,
A cry for the echoes
Coming off the canyon walls?

Out my window,
I watch the sky gather
Light;—stars, moon, planets—
Shine like the cottonwood leaves
Dancing with the shadows.
The night approaches,
Carrying a deeper domination of black.
I feel isolated and alone,
Until I remember
The songs of the coyotes.
It sounded like three of them.

NOTE ON MOONLIGHT

The moon rises over Cat Mesa,
Causing the quartz crystals in the canyon rock
Below Virgin Mesa to glow;
Night becomes a complex light, shining, reflecting.

All this is there to be seen,
If I look, and I do not have to look
Too deeply, beyond surfaces;
I only have to look in the right direction;

And if I look, reflection and shadow
Lift and enlarge and reveal
The existential presence of the canyon rocks
Until they become a sense rather than mere "things;"

And if I look in the right direction,
The sense displays power, evolves a life in itself,
And tricks of the mind discover purpose—
When the light meant only
That the world exists, there to be observed.

OF THE SURFACE OF THINGS

In this canyon, the Earth
        Remains larger than human comprehension,
But when I hike the trails
I know simple elements
Compose the world:
        Ponderosa-studded mesa top,
        Flesh-colored cliff walls,
        The dried-blood buttress
        Dotted with flame-shaped junipers,
        The thin ribbon of cottonwoods
        Over a flowing creek—
        All under a scarf of sky
        With gathering clouds.

From my window, I scan the invisible air
Where, I notice, the birds—
Ravens, vultures—and how the various shades of black
Conspire to create shadow.

The cottonwoods turn yellow.
Clouds fill the canyon with snow.
The sun hides in the drape of cloud.

THE SOLITUDE OF CATARACTS

Heraclitus spoke of rivers, and one of his fragments survived
through time, and since then, for two-thousand years,
the sight and sound of moving water remind humans
of his saying, and I repeat the sentiment often,
only using different words.

The creek flows down the canyon, unceasing but changing,
always, riffling reflections of ponderosas, then juniper
and pinyon, then cottonwoods, and then, finally, cane cholla,
in its descent. There is no apostrophe in the possessive of "it."

Moving water generates thought in which the natural
and the imagined become confused in a pleasant and comfortable
way. I often meditate to prolong the sensation.

I try to walk beside the creek every day, contemplating
how, beneath the glaring sun, eternity dwells
under the cottonwoods and locusts,
providing evidence, a reminder that I live
in a mortal universe.

My thoughts quiet with sudden realization,
then drift towards gratitude that the canyon wall
is made of hard rock that cracks and crumbles in time,
in its own time. There is no apostrophe in the possessive of "it."

WOMAN LOOKING AT A VASE OF FLOWERS

A painter's palette took living form,
Light and air clustered in blossoms,
In the same way the wind shapes birds,
Or clouds and rain gather in the flesh of plants.

The generalized expanse of sky
Particularized in the buds of *wisteria*;
Bricks and soil escaped abstraction
To bloom as incarnate *carnations*.
The skin of bowl fruit
Unfolded as fleshy roses.

No comparison to herself,
The colors—inhuman
Consolations of solace,
The gratitude of certainty—
Formed and fragrant in her senses.

WORLD WITHOUT PECULIARITY

Turning sixty-six. Another hot, glaring day.
My father sends a card, writes that he
Needs a new body, includes
A photo: me, aged four years.

Quiet all day. I don't care to talk.
Mom's been dead a decade, or more.
I'd have to find the death
Certificate to figure out how long it's been.

The cottonwoods stand ripe green
Over red sand. What
Does the poet mean by
"justified", "complete", and "end"?

Is it really "enough"?
I would argue the earth's value
Remains its inhumanity, and how
I perceive the moon at night:

Soaring over the poor red soil,
And how, on good days,
My bewilderment makes differences disappear;
I become myself, sure and true.

THINGS OF AUGUST, X

Evenings grow quiet, no more thunder or rain:
Another sign of the never-ending wonder of changing seasons.

The cottonwoods lose color, drop leaves,
Provide an awareness of leisurely decay.

Without clouds, the moon appears as a pale hand,
In a posture of greeting, signaling *farewell*.

Summer remains hot in the garden
With a fierce touch that wilts

And ripens. Providence precedes decay.
The cucumbers look worn out, a little weary.

TEA AT THE PALAZ OF HOON

Not less.
The sun traveled through
Purple clouds. Someone
Sprinkled corn in my beard.
I heard drums on my bones.
There were dancers—
Feathers, masks, hoops, songs.
Someone grabbed my hand,
Said, *Friendship*,
And pulled me into a circle.
Follow me.

I was the world in which I danced,
And there I found myself—
More truly and more strange.

AUTUMN REFRAIN

The tweet and twitter at dusk, completed,
And the swallows vanished,
And griefs of the sky,
The griefs of sky, too, disappeared…
The moon, and
Moon, contained
The dark orbit of bats
Singing song-less songs that I could not hear.
And yet in the quiet of
My solitude, remaining still,
Remaining and standing still,
Something dwelled:
A tweet and twitter of unheard song,
The creak of wings,
As bats dodged my body.

Standing still is the trick;
Being still, stillness,
Is the trick to mindful presence.

THE POEMS OF OUR CLIMATE

I
Gold and brown leaves float
On the still water of a stagnant pool;
The light under the trees, flecked with snow,
Reflects in the creek: a quiet storm
At the end of autumn (when evening
Starts soon after lunch).
Gold and brown leaves—did I
Expect more? The season itself
Reduces to the elemental: a white crust
Of snow, cold air, leafless trees,
Towering canyon walls—the rock streaked with ice—
The creek, where gold and brown leaves
Float on the surface, and nothing more.

II
Could the elemental erase my doubts,
Boil down my intrusive sense of self,
Make myself new in a drift of snow, or
In a pool of stagnant water?
Should I desire more, need more,
Than a canyon streaked with white snow?

III
No end to consciousness,
No cessation of the nostalgia
To remain myself. The canyon, me—
The lack of completion composes our perfection.
I sense the incompletion within me as a desire:
Its cure found in the awesome flaw of relationship:
The stagnant odors of still water and crusty snow surround
Gold and brown leaves that float
Under the shadow of rock streaked with ice.

THE AURORAS OF AUTUMN, II

Someone made an attempt to settle here...
Four walls of rock remain, ruins,
Above the creek, with mud
Of local color, call it "adobe,"
Still chinking the stone.
Four o'clocks grow at the base
Of one wall—
The canyon had rain this summer.
The wind piles red sand in a corner.

Stone and local color compose
Signs of invisibility, as if
Whoever built this was
Almost certain of failure.

I visit the place often:
It tops a favorite fishing hole.
In winter, it is a cold wind
That fills what seems to be
A shrunken canyon,
And clouds gather
To sometimes etch
Snow on the ledges of the canyon walls.
I turn my collar,
And cast with hunched shoulders.

THE SNOW MAN

I learned the voices of winter,
And recognized ice and the branches
Of ponderosas
Weighted with snow;

I have been chilled since birth.
Icicles drip from junipers,
And the cottonwoods shine

In the January morning. It is quiet,
The silence of the wind
In the leafless trees

Makes the sound of winter stillness,
Defines the fullness of vacancy.
Nothing.
I know nothing-ness.

NOT IDEAS ABOUT THE THING BUT THE THING ITSELF

Another long winter—
ice fractals on the insides
of windows, snow drifts,
mud smears on the entry mat.

One morning, the juncos
go missing at the feeder,
and the sun angles earlier
into my bedroom.

If I listen very well
I hear how that light,
as a still, small voice,
begins to sing.

When I walk outside:
seedlings top the soil with green,
leaves bud, pollen surrounds junipers
like a halo.

Like a new reality,
my senses apprehend spring.

TWO ILLUSTRATIONS THAT THE WORLD IS WHAT YOU MAKE OF IT, I

The ribbon of air between
The canyon walls seems to shrink
During winter, made more invisible
By the leafless cottonwoods.
The sky withers like the still creek in January.

It remains cold, of course, and
The angled light casts long shadows—
The sun seems farther away
And the distance reminds me
Of how the days grow shortened.

The wind, too, appears small
And quiet and low and weak.
I walk in the stillness
Of the clouds, dispossessed of ownership,
As is everyone, really—every man, woman.

This separation, me from the inhuman
World, forms a sense of identity,
But when I breathe the cold, still air
Of winter, I inspire another nature,
But only momentarily.

The cold air stirs the animal that is my body,
The senses that do not comprehend "outside of"
And "beyond," or a nature I
Am not part of, even
As my ears hear the church bell ring.

EXTRACTS FROM ADDRESSES TO THE ACADEMY OF FINE IDEAS, IV

Mid-April, on a day that
Arrived bright and still, almost warm,
I thought about the
Mesa-top and the ponderosas
That grow there.
It had been a long winter,
With cold since Thanksgiving,
When squalls of snow
Covered everything for weeks,
And now there was mud, a few
Tentative shoots of greenery,
With swelling buds on the cottonwoods,
And my eyes followed my thought,
Longingly, to the mesa
Above the shadow-streaked canyon walls.

It was spring: by afternoon
The wind blew, and I stood half-way
Up the trail to the mesa-top,
Stopping to breathe hard, and
I was not just somewhere, or anyplace,
But I rested *right* there on the trail
That barely managed to
Cling to the steep slope.
And then—I was,
Not just "one" or "a man."
I was myself again,
And I *still* wanted to see
The ponderosas that grow on the mesa-top.

Then, the wind drew clouds into the canyon,
And snow fell when I climbed past the
Rim rock into the forest of pine.
Snow piled, thinly, on tree branches;
Ice crystals hung on long needle clusters.

I walked in a fog
Of snowflake, in a drift of white
And gray and dark shapes.

This was the last snow
Of that long winter. Two days later
It was ninety degrees, and I stood in
Glaring light. On *that* day, all around me,
Life began to live again.
I was alive, and myself,
And thought it was time
To put in the garden.

BANAL SOJURN

The lemon tree droops with fruit
In its concrete tub on the front porch.
The sky remains the insistent blue
That warns of glaring light and stifling heat.
The cottonwoods hulk dark, motionless, still.
Fantail doves sing, a raven chortles.
Another summer day, when swell turns to wilt,
When monsoonal bloat withers,
When nothing reminds me of change,
But neither do I think of illness,
Of disease. This is not a sickness.

AN OLD MAN ASLEEP

Night. I sleep, the canyon rests;
Both: slumbering now in serious quiet.

Old man and canyon—think, feel,
Believe and doubt, relate within a singular drama;

The flesh-colors in the canyon rock
Reflect in the creek, move sleepily.

THE MEN THAT ARE FALLING

Summer. A hot moon, and
The sound of a cricket triggers
Forgotten memories.

Night winds enter through
The window. He does not sleep,
Lifts his head,

Thinks, *life itself*
Is the fulfillment
Of desire.

Laughs, speak only
Of what you know,
Doing what you do.

Closes his eyes, questions,
Can I love this earth enough
To die?

ANGLAIS MORT A FLORENCE

Comparison remains useless: each season
Marks another one, and one less to live through.
Every sound seems frail, and flat,
The world and I drift apart.

When I question my gratitude
And sense only doubt,
The lack of solace that
Identifies with faulty memory

Makes comparison useless:
To note that fewer stars populate the sky
Than last year, and that they shine
Less brightly, as do my own eyes.

The night grows dark, again, everyday—
But somehow I yield
Myself back to faith,
Solitary and open, giving myself

To one more breath,
Beyond compare.

Raised in southern California, dwelling on the redwood coast for most of his adult life, **Benjamin Green** recently displaced himself to New Mexico. A self-taught writer and artist, even his college major at Humboldt State University was self-designed. Green expresses his creativity through various visual mediums—watercolors, oil, enamel, broken fenceboards, poetry, fiction, creative nonfiction, and the personal essay. His literary work appears in journals from the southwest—*Sky Island Journal, Pinyon, Creosote*—as well as other print and online journals.

His previous publications include:

Poetry:
From a Greyhound Bus, The Lost Coast, Monologs from the Realm of Silence, This Coast of Many Colors, The Sound of Fish Dreaming, Keepers, and the upcoming *Old Man Looking through a Window at Night.*

Creative Non-Fiction and Personal Essays:
The Field Notes of a Madman, Barbless Hooks and Anchorholds, Until Only Silence Remains

Non-fiction
Beyond Roses are Red, Violets are Blue

Fiction:
From this Welter, Virgin Territory

He lives with Anita, his partner of more than thirty years, in Jemez Springs, New Mexico.

www.ingramcontent.com/pod-product-compliance
Lightning Source LLC
Chambersburg PA
CBHW022105080426
42734CB00009B/1491

9 7 9 8 8 9 9 9 0 1 9 0 4